SINGLE,
SOBER,
& SERIOUS...

SETTING BOUNDARIES & TRUSTING GOD'S PLAN

BY REBECCA BENSTON

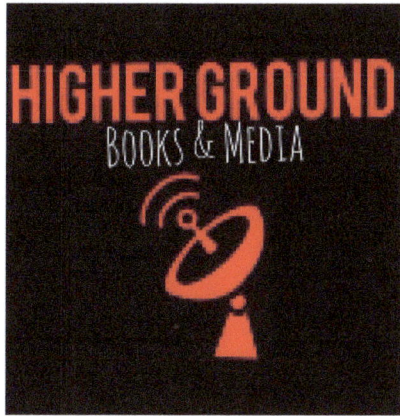

Higher Ground Books & Media
Springfield, Ohio.
http://highergroundbooksandmedia.com

Printed in the United States of America 2021

SINGLE, SOBER, & SERIOUS...

SETTING BOUNDARIES & TRUSTING GOD'S PLAN

BY REBECCA BENSTON

INTRODUCTION

There comes a time when we must decide what matters. Chasing relationships that offer nothing more than drama and the promise of something real cannot be a permanent state. I've put together some information for women who find themselves struggling to break free from relationships that offer no shelter, no commitment, and no value. Life is too short to waste on someone who sees you as an option. It's time to take inventory, stand up and declare that you are worth more than a part-time investment. It's time to get serious about your love life. Let's get started!

Rebecca Benston

FOREWORD

Some people have asked, "What's up with the bunny on the cover?" My answer is that the bunny symbolizes a couple of things. The first, a man that is basically refusing to grow up and take life seriously…or at least the relationship part. Note the dirty costume. It speaks to the lack of respect that some men have shown for me in relationships. Why would I ever want to be with someone like that? As he stands there, looking out over the water, he has finally come to the realization that I'm not coming back. No more chances for him.

The second symbol is my own ability to see the humor in some of the struggles I've faced. The picture adds a bit of irony to the theme of the book in that I knew I was dealing with some clowns when I dated them, yet I kept hoping that they would shape up. The dirty bunny could very well be the whimsical side of me, ever hopeful that my sense of humor could carry me through anything and finding that no matter how hard I tried, I couldn't make it work. At least not with the attitude I had at the time. Standing at the dock, looking out over yet another ship that has sailed, the bunny is at a loss. I've felt that way many times. But today, I'm finally able to shed the "costume" and continue my journey without feeling like a fool.

Either way, a transition has occurred. It didn't happen overnight. It didn't even happen over the course of a few years. But the important thing is that it happened.

CHAPTER ONE

For years, I thought that the problems I had in my relationships were all because I wasn't worthy of having a good man. I figured there had to be something wrong with me. After all, I had opinions and wanted my life to go somewhere. That kind of independence would be off-putting to any man, wouldn't it? So, I lowered my standards and found myself agreeing to things that I knew my spirit didn't agree with. I went along with the program and let the guys I dated call the shots. But I soon found that this lack of boundaries didn't serve me well either.

If we don't set standards for ourselves, we're likely to be pulled into any number of negative situations. This is especially true in relationships. For myself, I've typically been somewhat liberal in my selection criteria for romantic relationships. Although I know that I am smarter than this I've found myself entangled with some doozies over the years, so this year I made a conscious decision that I would no longer tolerate sub-standard interactions. Or to put it simply, no more losers. I've set some new criteria for myself and from this point on, if they don't measure up to these standards, they can keep on moving.

A good man won't be scared off by a strong, positive woman. A good man will appreciate your ability to think for yourself and to take care of business. A good man will be secure enough in his own character to see this kind of woman as an asset, a treasure of more value than gold. A man worthy of being a partner will know a woman of value when he sees it and he won't hesitate to let her know what she's worth to him.

Questions to consider as you read:

What are some common traits that I've been drawn to in past relationships?

1. _____
2. _____
3. _____
4. _____
5. _____
6. _____
7. _____

Which would you classify as being negative?

1. _____
2. _____
3. _____
4. _____

Do you feel that you share any of those traits?

_____ Yes

_____ No

Single - Not separated, not part of the way out of a relationship, not delusional about their status...but SINGLE. For further definition, this means that you do not share a home or any other living space with another female who acts in the capacity of a mate. You are not estranged from your spouse and waiting until you have enough money for a divorce. You are not in any kind of relationship with any other woman who considers themselves to be your significant other. There is no other woman, or God forbid, man who considers themselves to be your lover, girlfriend, boyfriend, common law spouse, shack job, steady, partner or your mate. In short, when you go to bed at night, you are alone. When you make decisions about things, there is no other person who should have a say in things. No one else's children are calling you Dad or thinking of you as the man in the house. You are not romantically entangled with anyone else in any way. This is what single means.

#HigherGroundforLife

CHAPTER TWO

The first standard that a man must meet is that he must, and I mean ABSOLUTELY MUST be single. Not separated, not part of the way out of a relationship, not delusional about your status…but SINGLE. For further definition, this means that you do not share a home or any other living space with another female who acts in the capacity of a mate. You are not estranged from your spouse and waiting until you have enough money for a divorce. You are not in any kind of relationship with any other woman who considers themselves to be your significant other. There is no other woman, or God forbid, man who considers themselves to be your lover, girlfriend, boyfriend, common law spouse, shack job, steady, partner or your mate. In short, when you go to bed at night, you are alone. When you make decisions about things, there is no other person who should have a say in things. No one else's children are calling you Dad or thinking of you as the man in the house. You are not romantically entangled with anyone else in any way. This is what single means. It's not difficult, but it is an absolute necessity if you are going to be in a relationship with me.

It may seem that there is some wiggle room here, but really, all that we can really count on with that "wiggle" room is that he will never fully commit to us if he is still on the fence about his standing with the other woman. There is no good reason to allow him the freedom to have one foot in her pasture and the other in ours. And if he would go that far, he would go as far as to have more than just one other woman on the hook. In many cases, he probably has three or four ladies lined up to meet whatever needs he decides he has at any given time.

Be watchful. *The Little Black Book of Big Red Flags* by Natasha Burton, Julie Fishman, and Meagan McCrary gives several examples of things he may do that reveal when you are not his one and only one and only. These two definitely apply.

> "He's shady with his phone" – this is probably the biggest indicator that he's hiding something or someone from you. A man who is honest and faithful doesn't need to hide his phone, he doesn't need to hide his text messages, and he doesn't need to have a bunch of numbers and contact information for other women if he's serious about you. If he's not willing to share this information with you or if he's suspiciously secretive about the calls he takes, he's likely talking or texting someone who is in direct competition with you for his affections.

> "He's inflexible with his time" - My interpretation of this is that you may find that it is difficult to reach him at a certain time of day. Maybe he cuts off all communication with you at around 4 or 5 p.m.; maybe you never hear from him at night. Maybe, you only hear from him during working hours. This may well be because during the hours when he should be home and available to talk, he has a significant other nearby and he can't risk the communication. Check his patterns. If something seems fishy, then it most likely is. Trust that little voice inside that tells you there's something off about this guy's communication habits. That little voice is loud for a reason and it's telling you that he is anything but single.

Sober - *By sober, I mean that you don't need alcohol to get through your day, week, or most difficult situations you encounter. I understand that sometimes people like to have a drink, but I don't want someone for whom drinking alcohol is a regular part of their daily routine. I was a heavy drinker for a brief period of time and I grew up with an alcoholic in the house. I don't want that in my life. I don't handle my problems by staying liquored up and I don't expect my partner to do that either. I expect that when we talk, you'll be lucid. Your decisions will be solid because you aren't under the influence of three to ten beers or shots. You won't just show up when you need someplace to crash because you drank too much and my house is closer than yours. If you can't approach life responsibly, then I have no time or use for you. I need someone who can handle life and its challenges. Someone who doesn't hide inside a bottle when things get tough. If you see your bartender more than you see me, then this just won't work.* #HigherGroundforLife

CHAPTER THREE

The second standard is that you must be sober. By sober, I mean that you don't need alcohol or drugs to get through your day, week, or most difficult situations you encounter. I understand that sometimes people like to have a drink, but I don't want someone for whom drinking alcohol is a regular part of their daily routine. I was a heavy drinker for a brief period of time, and I grew up with an alcoholic in the house. I don't want that in my life. I don't handle my problems by staying liquored up and I don't expect my partner to do that either. I expect that when we talk, you'll be lucid. Your decisions will be solid because you aren't under the influence of three to ten beers or shots. You won't just show up when you need someplace to crash because you drank too much, and my house is closer than yours. If you can't approach life responsibly, then I have no time or use for you. I need someone who can handle life and its challenges. Someone who doesn't hide inside a bottle when things get tough. If you see your bartender more than you see me, then this just won't work.

Addiction is serious business. I know better than anyone that when you're under the constant influence of alcohol, you can't make good decisions and you probably aren't even interested in doing so. At the point where the thing you look forward to is your next happy hour, you've lost your direction. God didn't create us to slowly kill ourselves with overindulgence in alcohol or drugs. And even if you believe that there's nothing wrong with daily alcohol intake, the degree to which your decision-making is impacted by substances will be evident in the fruit you produce. I shouldn't have to lecture a grown man on when it makes sense to put down the bottle. And as long as he is able to handle his business without being disrespectful to me or acting recklessly, I won't say a word. But if your behavior begins to worry me or worse, threaten my personal safety and security, you'll be out faster than you can say, "But, baby."

If you are dealing with addiction and you need help, call the Substance Abuse and Mental Health Services Administration (SAMHSA) at 1-800-662-4357

Other Recovery Resources:

Knowing Affliction and Doing Recovery: How to Overcome Addictions, Mental Illness, and PTSD with the Dayton Model by John Baldasare

From a Hole in My Life to a Life Made Whole by Janet Kay Teresa

Out of Darkness by Stephen Bowman

Serious - *By this I don't mean that you can never crack a smile. I'm a joker at heart and I love to laugh, but when it comes to relationships I don't want to be the butt of your joke. Being serious means that you care enough about me to include me in all parts of your life and that there are no special friends out there that I don't know about. You're not more involved with sports or cars or anything else than you are in our relationship. It is important to have interests outside the relationship, but if there are things you do that take up more of your time, energy, and resources than I do I'm going to have to question why I'm even in the equation. I'm a grown woman and if you have to date two or three people at a time to be able to figure out which one you like best, I'm not interested in being in that lineup.*

RB

#HigherGroundforLife

CHAPTER FOUR

The last major standard is that you must be serious. By this I don't mean that you can never crack a smile. I'm a joker at heart and I love to laugh, but when it comes to relationships, I don't want to be the butt of your joke. Being serious means that you care enough about me to include me in all parts of your life and that there are no special friends out there that I don't know about. You're not more involved with sports or cars or anything else than you are in our relationship.

It is important to have interests outside the relationship, but if there are things you do that take up more of your time, energy, and resources than I do I'm going to have to question why I'm even in the equation. When someone asks you about your relationship, you can definitively say that you are in a relationship with me. There should be no question about whether or not we're headed toward marriage. If we are in a relationship, then that is my intention. I am too old to waste time on flings. What appealed to me in my twenties no longer works. I'm a grown woman and if you have to date two or three people at a time to be able to figure out which one you like best, I'm not interested in being included in that lineup. If I'm taking the time to entertain you, then at least have the courtesy to approach the relationship like a grown man. Playtime is over and I just don't have time for all that mess.

I'm a good woman and I deserve someone who is willing and able to be a good man. I don't need or want a relationship at the moment, but I'm not closed off to the idea of having one if the right person appears. The thing is, there have always been a few guys who wanted to hang around and see what they could get from me without actually offering anything in return.

In my youth, I was more likely to put up with this behavior, but the older I get the less likely I am to deal with this. If you want a relationship, don't mess around with someone's emotions. For the most part, if a woman has been taking care of herself and, if it applies, her children doesn't want to take on another person that she has to treat like a child. If she is open to "dating" you, she is hoping that you will at least be able to stand on your own two feet and that she'll be able to trust you when you are out of her sight. If you're still playing games, then stick to the bar scene or whatever ridiculousness you've been involved in. You're obviously not ready for prime time. In any case, I look forward to a life free from the distraction of men who still want to act like children. I should be able to get quite a bit done.

CHAPTER FIVE

I don't want to end this book without saying that having a man in your life isn't always necessary. Some women are content living their lives without that sort of companionship. And there is absolutely nothing wrong with being your own best friend. Just don't feel that you have to settle for less than the best when it comes to picking a life partner. It truly is better to be on your own than to be weighed down by the burden of suspicion, mistrust, and inconsistent interest. We are made for better, and we need to remind ourselves of this on at least a daily basis.

Handle your business, ladies. God has a plan for you, and it doesn't include being jerked around by a man-child. When He has prepared someone for you, He'll send him your way. In the meantime, keep preparing yourself so that you'll be able to identify him when he does show up.

EMPOWERING BIBLE VERSES FOR WOMEN

Luke 1:45
"And blessed is she that believed: for there shall be a performance of those things which were told her from the Lord."

Proverbs 11:16
"A gracious woman retaineth honour: and strong men retain riches."

Proverbs 31:30
Charm is deceptive, and beauty is fleeting; but a woman who fears the Lord is to be praised.

Psalm 20:4-5
"May He give you the desires of your heart and make all of your plans succeed. May we shout for joy... May the Lord grant all of your requests."

Psalm 46:5
"God is in the midst of her; she shall not be moved: God shall help her, and that right early."

The Entire Book of Ruth
The Entire Book of Esther

JOURNAL/NOTES PAGES

FOR ANY INSIGHTS YOU CARE TO RECORD

_____

_____

_____

_____

_____

_____

_____

_____

_____

_____

_____

_____

_____

_____

_____

_____

_____

_____

_____

_____

_____

_____

_____

_____

_____

_____

_____

_____

_____

_____

_____

_____

OTHER RESOURCES:

Helpful Titles Available from Higher Ground Books & Media

Don't Be Stupid (And I Mean That in the Nicest Way) by Rebecca Benston

Feed Your Soul Journal by Higher Ground Books & Media

Fill Your Cup by Deborah Armstrong Bryant

From Judgment to Jubilee by Rebecca Benston

Overcomer Student Manual by Rev. Forrest Henslee

Seven Day Devotional Series by Rebecca Benston

The Deliverance Series by Yasmin S. Brown

The Reconstruction Journal by Yasmin S. Brown

Wise Up to Rise Up by Rebecca Benston

Also Available on Amazon

Codependent No More by Melanie Beattie

No Matter What: 9 Steps to Living the Life You Love by Lisa Nichols

The Little Black Book of Big Red Flags by Natasha Burton, Julie Fishman, and Meagan McCrary

The Survivor Personality: Why Some People Are Stronger, Smarter, and More Skillful at Handling Life's Difficulties by Al Siebert, PhD

Other titles from Higher Ground Books & Media:

Raven Transcending Fear by Terri Kozlowski

The Power of Knowing by Jean Walters

Forgiven and Not Forgotten by Terra Kern

Through the Sliver of a Frosted Window by Robin Melet

Breaking the Cycle by Willie Deeanjlo White

Healing in God's Power by Yvonne Green

Chronicles of a Spiritual Journey by Stephen Shepherd

The Real Prison Diaries by Judy Frisby

The Words of My Father by Mark Nemetz

The Bottom of This by Tramaine Hannah

Add these titles to your collection today!

http://www.highergroundbooksandmedia.com

Do you have a story to tell?

Higher Ground Books & Media is an independent Christian-based publisher specializing in stories of triumph! Our purpose is to empower, inspire, and educate through the sharing of personal experiences.

Please visit our website for our submission guidelines.

http://www.highergroundbooksandmedia.com